JOE MONTANA, HUGH MCELHENNY, JOE PERRY, JERRY RICE, TERRELL OWENS, BRENT JONES, HARRIS BARTON, BOB ST. CLAIR, GUY MCINTYRE, RANDY CROSS, FORREST BLUE, FRED DEAN, CEDRICK HARDMAN, BRYANT YOUNG, LEO NOMELLINI, PATRICK WILLIS, CHARLES HALEY, DAVE WILCOX, JIMMY JOHNSON, ERIC WRIGHT, RONNIE LOTT, MERTON

THE STORY OF THE SAN FRANCISCO 49ERS

HANKS, RAY WERSCHING, TOMMY DAVIS, JOE MONTANA, HUGH MCELHENNY, JOE PERRY, JERRY RICE, TERRELL OWENS, BRENT JONES, HARRIS BARTON, BOB ST. CLAIR, GUY MCINTYRE, RANDY CROSS

THE STORY OF THE SAN FRANCISCO 49ERS

BY JIM WHITING

CREATIVE EDUCATION / CREATIVE PAPERBACKS

PUBLISHED BY CREATIVE EDUCATION AND CREATIVE PAPERBACKS
P.O. BOX 227, MANKATO, MINNESOTA 56002
CREATIVE EDUCATION AND CREATIVE PAPERBACKS ARE IMPRINTS OF THE
CREATIVE COMPANY
WWW.THECREATIVECOMPANY.US

DESIGN AND PRODUCTION BY BLUE DESIGN (WWW.BLUEDES.COM)
ART DIRECTION BY RITA MARSHALL
PRINTED IN CHINA

PHOTOGRAPHS BY CORBIS (BETTMANN), GETTY IMAGES (BRIAN BAHR, ROBERT
BECK/SI, JOHN BIEVER/SI, MIKE EHRMANN, JAMES FLORES, FOCUS ON SPORT,
DANIEL GLUSKOTER/ICON SPORTSWIRE, GEORGE GOJKOVICH, OTTO GREULE JR./
ALLSPORT, WALTER IOOSS JR./SI, JED JACOBSOHN, HEINZ KLUETMEIER/SI,
KIRBY LEE/NFL, RONALD MARTINEZ/ALLSPORT, NHAT V. MEYER/MEDIANEWS
GROUP/MERCURY NEWS, MPS/NFL, FRANK RIPPON/NFL, GEORGE ROSE, PAUL
SPINELLI, KEVIN TERRELL, TONY TOMSIC/NFL, GREG TROTT, MICHAEL ZAGARIS,
MICHAEL ZAGARIS/SAN FRANCISCO 49ERS)

NAMES: WHITING, JIM, AUTHOR.
TITLE: THE STORY OF THE SAN FRANCISCO 49ERS / JIM WHITING.
SERIES: NFL TODAY.
INCLUDES INDEX.
SUMMARY: THIS HIGH-INTEREST HISTORY OF THE NATIONAL FOOTBALL
LEAGUE'S SAN FRANCISCO 49ERS HIGHLIGHTS MEMORABLE GAMES,
SUMMARIZES SEASONAL TRIUMPHS AND DEFEATS, AND FEATURES STANDOUT
PLAYERS SUCH AS JOE MONTANA.
IDENTIFIERS: LCCN 2018060965 / ISBN 978-1-64026-157-0 (HARDCOVER) / ISBN
978-1-62832-720-5 (PBK) / ISBN 978-1-64000-275-3 (EBOOK)
SUBJECTS: LCSH: SAN FRANCISCO 49ERS (FOOTBALL TEAM)—HISTORY—
JUVENILE LITERATURE.
CLASSIFICATION: LCC GV956.S3 W55 2019 / DDC 796.332/640979461—DC23

FIRST EDITION HC 9 8 7 6 5 4 3 2 1
FIRST EDITION PBK 9 8 7 6 5 4 3 2 1

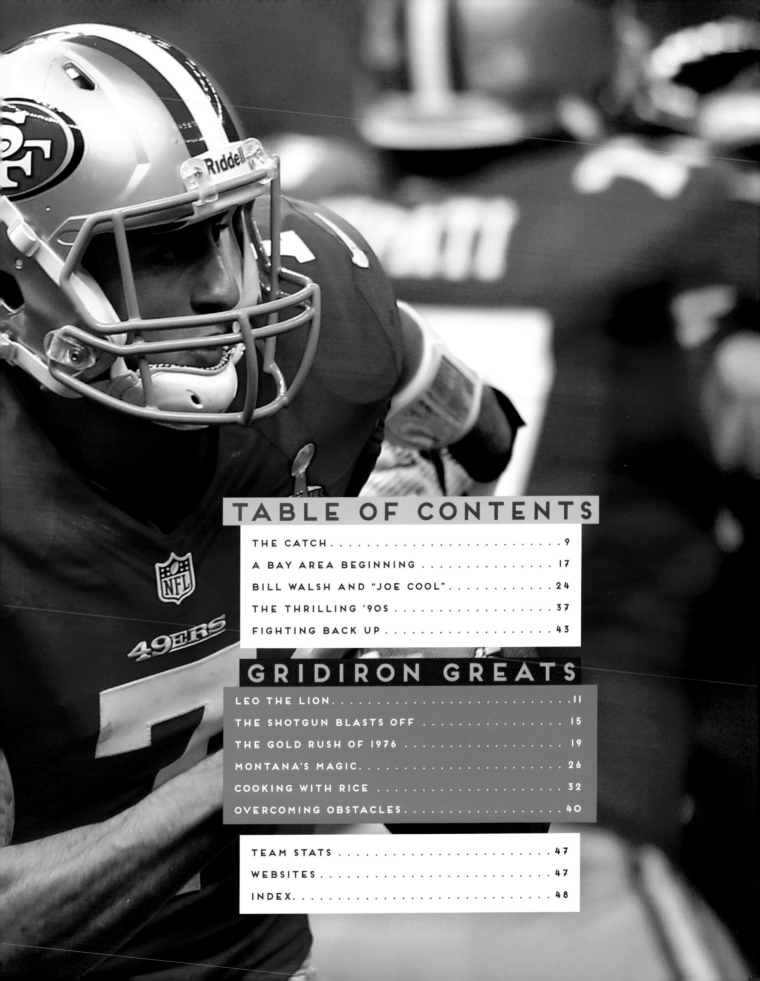

TABLE OF CONTENTS

GRIDIRON GREATS

THE CATCH

During the 1970s, the San Francisco 49ers ranked among the worst teams in the National Football League (NFL). The 49ers finally turned things around in 1981. They won 13 games. They made the playoffs for the first time in nine years. San Francisco easily defeated the New York Giants in the divisional round.

Next, the 49ers faced the Dallas Cowboys in the National Football Conference (NFC) Championship Game. The winner would advance to Super Bowl XVI. Dallas had dominated the NFC since 1970. It had appeared in five Super Bowls. It had also crushed San Francisco, 59–14, the previous season. The 49ers returned the favor in 1981 with a 45–14 win. Still, many Dallas players suggested that the "real" Cowboys had not shown up to that game.

SAN FRANCISCO 49ERS

9

LEFT: COACH BILL WALSH

The NFC Championship Game was another story. The 49ers scored first. Then there were five lead changes. San Francisco had nearly 400 yards of offense. Dallas had just 250. But the 49ers committed six turnovers. The Cowboys had a 27–21 lead late in the game. San Francisco quarterback Joe Montana led his team downfield. Less than a minute remained. The 49ers had the ball on the Dallas six-yard line.

Montana took the snap. He rolled to his right. Several Dallas defenders pressured him. They nearly tackled him. He managed to pass into the end zone toward receiver

LEO NOMELLINI
DEFENSIVE/OFFENSIVE TACKLE

49ERS SEASONS: 1950–63
HEIGHT: 6-FOOT-3
WEIGHT: 259 POUNDS

GRIDIRON GREATS
LEO THE LION

Leo Nomellini was born in Italy. Then he moved with his family to Chicago. As a teen, he worked to help support his family. He had no time for sports. He began playing football in the Marine Corps during World War II. He went on to a successful college football career. He was nicknamed "The Lion." A teammate explained, "When he'd come around the corner, he would just roar." He became All-Pro on both sides of the ball. During the off-season, he was a professional wrestler. "He was as strong as three bulls," said teammate Joe Perry. "He'd slap you on the back and knock you 20 feet."

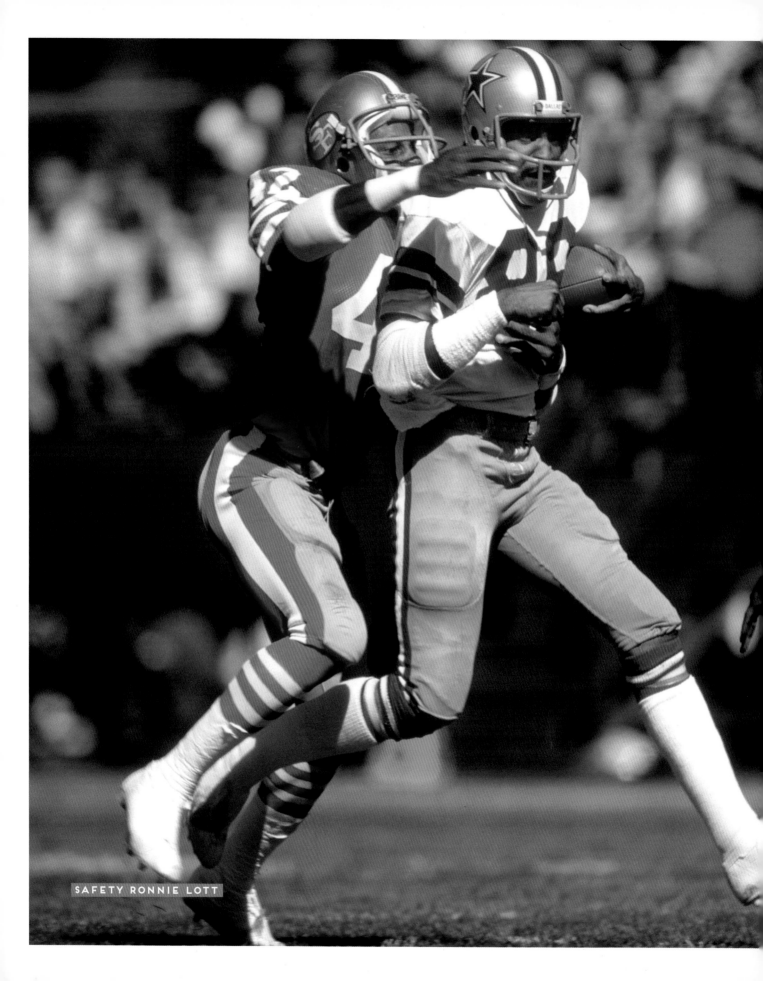

SAFETY RONNIE LOTT

"I REMEMBER SEEING THE BALL COMING AND THINKING, 'WOW, THAT'S PRETTY HIGH.'"

Dwight Clark. "[Cowboys defensive back] Everson Walls was right beside me; he had me covered," Clark said. "I remember seeing the ball coming and thinking, 'Wow, that's pretty high.'" But Clark, who stood 6-foot-4, leaped as high as he could. He barely touched the ball with his fingertips. It was enough to secure the ball for a touchdown. The 49ers kicked the extra point. San Francisco won, 28–27.

The play became known as "The Catch." It propelled the 49ers to the first of four Super Bowl wins during the 1980s. It often appears in lists of the 10 greatest individual plays in NFL history.

SAN FRANCISCO 49ERS

13

QUARTERBACK ALEX SMITH AND
CENTER ERIC HEITMANN

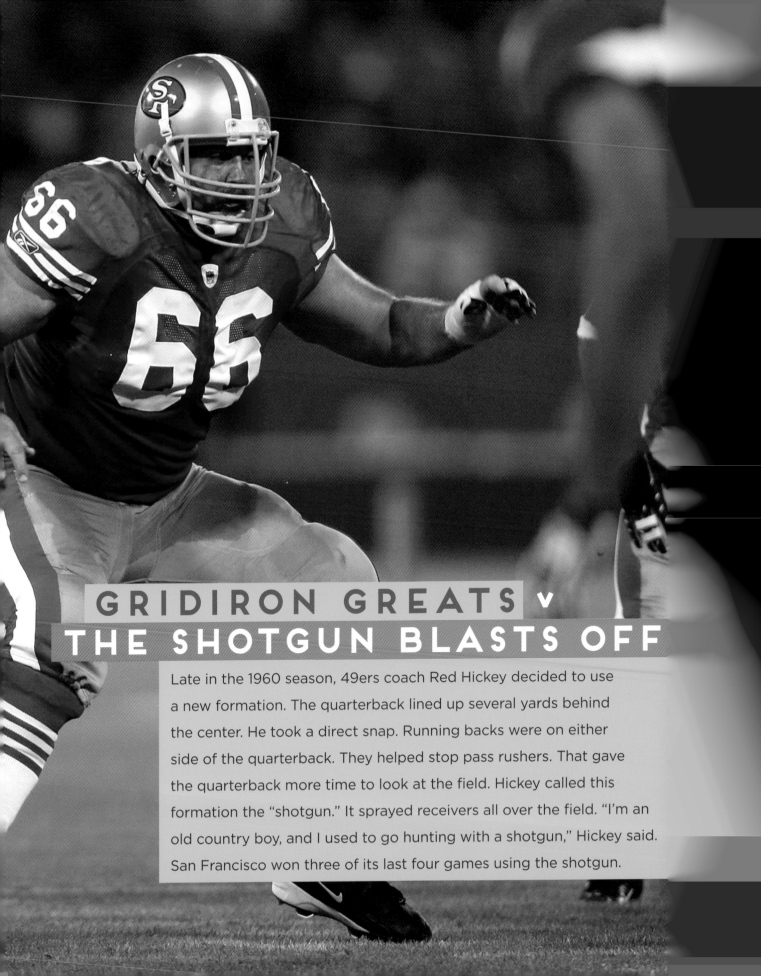

GRIDIRON GREATS ∨
THE SHOTGUN BLASTS OFF

Late in the 1960 season, 49ers coach Red Hickey decided to use a new formation. The quarterback lined up several yards behind the center. He took a direct snap. Running backs were on either side of the quarterback. They helped stop pass rushers. That gave the quarterback more time to look at the field. Hickey called this formation the "shotgun." It sprayed receivers all over the field. "I'm an old country boy, and I used to go hunting with a shotgun," Hickey said. San Francisco won three of its last four games using the shotgun.

A BAY AREA BEGINNING

n the early 1940s, San Francisco trucking company executive Anthony Morabito wanted to join the NFL. When the league denied his request, Morabito and his brother, Victor, formed a team in the All-America Football Conference (AAFC). The team began playing in 1946. Naming the franchise was easy. In 1848, rich deposits of gold had been discovered near San Francisco. Thousands of miners hoped to strike gold. They swarmed into the area. They were nicknamed "49ers" for the year they arrived.

The 49ers' first coach was Buck Shaw. He assembled a talented lineup. Quarterback Frankie Albert led the team.

61 SACKS IN 1976

SAN FRANCISCO 49ERS

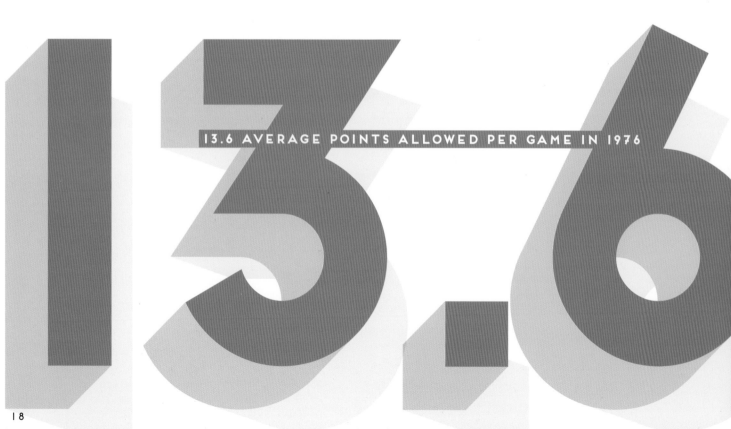

13.6 AVERAGE POINTS ALLOWED PER GAME IN 1976

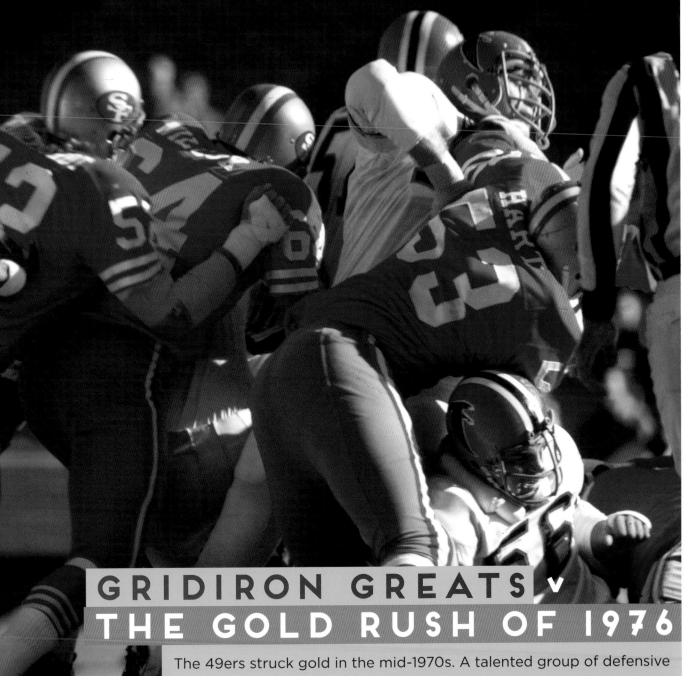

GRIDIRON GREATS
THE GOLD RUSH OF 1976

The 49ers struck gold in the mid-1970s. A talented group of defensive linemen came together for a record-setting season. Tommy Hart (pictured) and Cedrick Hardman were the defensive ends. Cleveland Elam and Jimmy Webb played tackle. This unit earned the nickname "Gold Rush." In 1976, the Gold Rush was a defensive wall. It limited opposing offenses to just 13 passing touchdowns for the year. They set a team record with 61 quarterback sacks. The group's best game came against the undefeated Los Angeles Rams. The 49ers shut out the Rams, 16–0. They sacked quarterback James Harris 10 times.

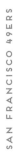

Running back/defensive back Len Eshmont and guard Bruno Banducci were key players. The 49ers put together a combined record of 38–14–2 in four AAFC seasons. Unfortunately, the Cleveland Browns were even better. Cleveland won the league championship each year.

The AAFC folded in 1949. The NFL absorbed the 49ers. The Browns and the Baltimore Colts also joined the NFL. San Francisco went just 3–9 in 1950. From 1951 to 1954, the 49ers posted winning records. Their star players included defensive tackle/offensive tackle Leo Nomellini. Hugh "The King" McElhenny and Joe "The Jet" Perry carried the ball. Albert gave Perry his nickname. "When that guy comes by to take a handoff, his slipstream darn near knocks you over," he said. "He's strictly jet-propelled." In 1953 and 1954, Perry became the first player to rush for more than 1,000 yards in back-to-back seasons.

By then, Y. A. Tittle had become quarterback. Tittle, McElhenny, Perry, and running back John Henry Johnson became known as the "Million Dollar Backfield." Tittle also had a standout receiver. R. C. Owens was a former basketball star. The quarterback threw "alley-oop" passes to Owens. He would soar over defenders to snag the ball. "It's the strangest thing I've ever seen on a football field," one reporter noted.

In 1957, rookie quarterback John Brodie gave fans a glimpse of his potential. He filled in for the injured Tittle in a game against the Colts. In the final minute, Brodie threw the game-winning touchdown pass. The 49ers went 8–4 on the season. They made their first trip to the

Y. A. TITTLE AND JOHN BRODIE

[TITTLE] THREW "ALLEY-OOP" PASSES TO OWENS. HE WOULD SOAR OVER DEFENDERS TO SNAG THE BALL.

playoffs. They lost to the Detroit Lions.

The 49ers often had respectable records in the 1960s. But they never reached the playoffs. That decade featured the start of the "shotgun" formation. To run it, the quarterback had to be able to scramble away from would-be tacklers. Brodie was more mobile than Tittle. "I held John off until the shotgun," Tittle later admitted.

Coach Red Hickey further confused opponents. He rotated quarterbacks. He sometimes replaced Brodie with Billy Kilmer. In 1961, Kilmer passed for a modest 286 yards. But he rushed for a whopping 509. He scored four rushing touchdowns in one game against the Minnesota Vikings. It was a team record.

JOHN BRODIE

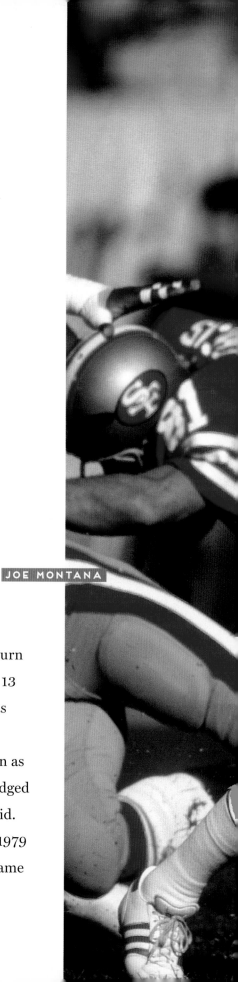

BILL WALSH AND "JOE COOL"

JOE MONTANA

San Francisco seemed to turn a corner in 1970. The 49ers made the postseason for the first time in 13 years. They did the same thing in the next two seasons. But the Dallas Cowboys knocked them out each time. Years of frustration followed.

In 1978, San Francisco hired Bill Walsh as coach. He had a reputation as a great offensive mind. "When I took over the 49ers, we were acknowledged as the least-talented, least-experienced franchise in the NFL," Walsh said. The 49ers selected quarterback Joe Montana in the third round of the 1979 NFL Draft. They took a year to prepare him for the NFL. Montana became

GRIDIRON GREATS
MONTANA'S MAGIC

NFL scouts wondered if Joe Montana's arm was strong enough to play professional football. But 49ers coach Bill Walsh recognized his talents. "The minute I saw Joe move, there was no question in my mind that he was the best I'd seen," said Walsh. "I knew with the offense I planned to run, Joe would be great." Walsh was right. Montana guided his team to nine playoff berths. He led the way to four Super Bowl titles. His "Montana Magic" helped the 49ers come from behind in the fourth quarter to win 31 times. "Joe Cool" was always calm under pressure.

JOE MONTANA
QUARTERBACK

49ERS SEASONS: 1979-92
HEIGHT: 6-FOOT-2
WEIGHT: 200 POUNDS

SAN FRANCISCO 49ERS

the starter during the 1980 season. The 49ers made national headlines late in the season. They trailed the New Orleans Saints, 35–7, at halftime. San Francisco roared back. The 49ers won, 38–35, in overtime. It was the biggest comeback in NFL history up to that point. But San Francisco finished the season with just six wins.

By now, though, Walsh had assembled a star-studded roster. It included Montana and receiver Dwight Clark. In 1981, the team drafted hard-hitting safety Ronnie Lott. Another key player was veteran linebacker Jack "Hacksaw" Reynolds. He earned his nickname in college. He used a hacksaw to cut a car in half. Walsh noted that the nickname also fit Reynolds's playing style, "because he cut people down."

The pieces came together that year. The 49ers went 13–3. They beat the Cowboys for the NFC championship. In Super Bowl XVI, they faced the Cincinnati Bengals. The 49ers led 20–0 at halftime. They held on to win 26–21.

DWIGHT CLARK

The 49ers were finally champions!

The following season was a letdown. But the Niners came back strong in 1983. They finished 10–6. The Washington Redskins knocked them out of the playoffs. But the 49ers were about to strike gold. In 1984, they beat the Miami Dolphins 38–16 in Super Bowl XIX. They topped the Bengals 20–16 four years later in Super Bowl XXIII.

RONNIE LOTT

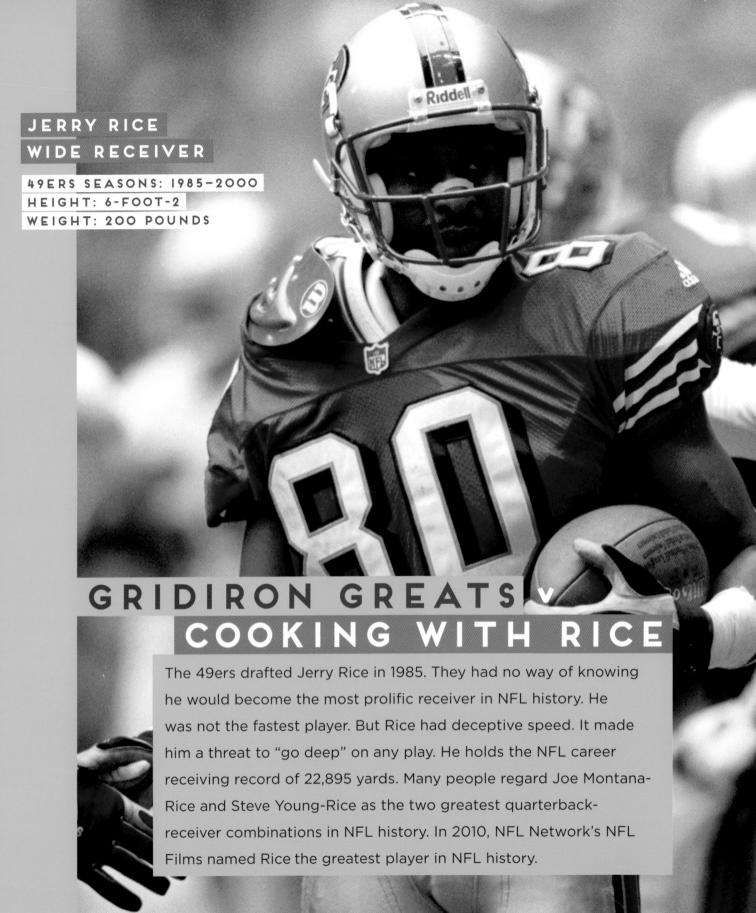

49ERS SEASONS: 1985–2000
HEIGHT: 6-FOOT-2
WEIGHT: 200 POUNDS

GRIDIRON GREATS v
COOKING WITH RICE

The 49ers drafted Jerry Rice in 1985. They had no way of knowing he would become the most prolific receiver in NFL history. He was not the fastest player. But Rice had deceptive speed. It made him a threat to "go deep" on any play. He holds the NFL career receiving record of 22,895 yards. Many people regard Joe Montana-Rice and Steve Young-Rice as the two greatest quarterback-receiver combinations in NFL history. In 2010, NFL Network's NFL Films named Rice the greatest player in NFL history.

197

303

197 CAREER RECEIVING TOUCHDOWNS

303 GAMES PLAYED

Montana received much of the credit for this dynasty. He was nicknamed "Joe Cool." He stayed calm in tough situations. He was surrounded by great players. Running back Roger Craig could run and catch. In 1985, he was the first player to amass more than 1,000 yards rushing and 1,000 yards receiving in the same season. Jerry Rice emerged as a top-notch receiver. He led the league in receiving yardage and touchdowns six times.

Walsh retired early in 1989 after the Super Bowl win over Cincinnati. Assistant coach George Seifert replaced him. Under Seifert, Montana enjoyed the best season of his career. In 1989, he passed for 3,521 yards. He threw 26 touchdowns passes. He was even better in Super Bowl XXIV against the Denver Broncos. He threw five touchdown passes. Montana started feeling sorry for Denver. "To have it go that well in a Super Bowl makes the game fun," said Montana, "but you get to a point when you start thinking about what it must be like to be on the other side."

THE THRILLING '90S

In 1990, the 49ers lost in the NFC Championship Game. The Giants kicked the game-winning field goal as time ran out. The following season, Montana suffered an elbow injury. He could not play. The team looked to backup quarterback Steve Young. He had joined the 49ers in 1987. Although he had been in the background, his physical talents were obvious. He could scramble to pick up extra yards. He could throw with great accuracy, even on the run.

San Francisco continued to win. In 1992, the 49ers went 14–2. It was the best record in the league. But they lost to the Cowboys in the conference championship. The following year, the 49ers went 10–6. They returned to the playoffs. They crushed the Giants, 44–3. Running back Ricky Watters ran

for five touchdowns. That set an NFL single-game playoff record. Unfortunately, the Cowboys stopped their Super Bowl run. Dallas beat San Francisco in the NFC title game.

Everything fell into place for San Francisco in 1994. It went 13–3. Rice set team records. He had 112 receptions for 1,499 yards. He caught 13 touchdowns. The 49ers roared into the playoffs. This time, they beat the Cowboys for the NFC title. They headed to Super Bowl XXIX. They met the San Diego Chargers. Young tossed a Super Bowl–record six touchdown passes. He led the 49ers to a 49–26 win.

The 49ers fought their way to 11–5 in 1995. Defense was the team's strength. But the Green Bay Packers bounced San Francisco from the playoffs. One year later, the two teams met again in the playoffs. Turnovers plagued the 49ers. They lost again.

In 1997, Steve Mariucci became San Francisco's coach. He led the 49ers to an 11-game winning streak. In the postseason, San Francisco again fell to Green Bay.

The 49ers remained among the NFL's elite in 1998. Yet again they faced the Packers in the playoffs. With only eight seconds left, Young rifled a 25-yard touchdown strike to receiver Terrell Owens. It was called "The Catch II." San Francisco won, 30–27. The next week, however, the Atlanta Falcons inched past them, 20–18.

In 1999, Young suffered his fourth concussion in three years. He had to retire. San Francisco plummeted to 4–12. It was the club's first losing season in 17 years. Jeff Garcia took over at quarterback. He passed for a team-record 4,278 yards in 2000.

Owens became Garcia's main target. In a game against the Chicago Bears in December, "T. O." pulled in 20 receptions. That set a new NFL record. "He's big, he can run, and if you play him one-on-one, he can outjump a defensive back," said St. Louis Rams defensive coordinator Lovie Smith. "He's the complete package."

JEFF GARCIA

FRANK GORE
RUNNING BACK

49ERS SEASONS: 2005-14
HEIGHT: 5-FOOT-9
WEIGHT: 212 POUNDS

GRIDIRON GREATS ˅
OVERCOMING OBSTACLES

Frank Gore grew up in a two-bedroom house. He lived there with nine other family members. He had dyslexia, a severe learning problem. It almost kept him from going to college. His mother abused drugs. Later, she developed kidney disease. He became her primary caregiver. Gore suffered two serious knee injuries playing college football. He hurt his shoulder in his rookie year. But Gore never gave up. As he said later, "I think it all happened for a reason. I think what I went through made me appreciate the game even more." San Francisco fans certainly appreciated Gore. He became the team's all-time career rushing leader.

64

64 RUSHING TOUCHDOWNS WITH THE 49ERS

148

148 GAMES PLAYED WITH THE 49ERS

FIGHTING BACK UP

The 49ers reached the playoffs in 2001. However, Green Bay once again beat them. In 2002, San Francisco returned to the playoffs. The Giants led, 38–14, late in the third quarter. Then the 49ers charged back. They completed one of the biggest comebacks in NFL postseason history. They scored 25 unanswered points to win 39–38. Unfortunately, they could not muster the same magic the next week. They lost to the Tampa Bay Buccaneers.

The 49ers dropped to 7–9 in 2003. After that, they struggled. Rookie Frank Gore put in a solid season in 2005. He led the team in rushing yards. In 2006, Gore rumbled for 1,695 rushing yards. It was a franchise record.

The 49ers entered 2007 with high hopes. But injuries derailed the season. They won only five games. Rookie linebacker Patrick Willis provided one of the few highlights. He made 135 tackles. He earned NFL Defensive Rookie of the Year honors.

In 2008, new coach Mike Singletary endeared himself to fans. "Our formula is this: We go out, we hit people in the mouth," he said. The team won five of its final eight games that season. It finished 7–9. The 49ers improved to 8–8 the following year. Then they finished the next season 6–10. Singletary was fired.

Jim Harbaugh took over as coach in 2011. He had led nearby Stanford University to national prominence. The 49ers stunned fans with a 13–3 record. One key to this turnaround was the improved play of quarterback Alex Smith. He had been the first overall selection in the 2005 NFL Draft. But he struggled in his first few NFL years. In the postseason, the 49ers hosted the Saints in the divisional round. It was a thrilling contest. San Francisco trailed with nine seconds left. Smith fired a 14-yard touchdown to tight end Vernon Davis. It was called "The Catch III." The 49ers won, 36–32. Unfortunately, San Francisco's march toward the Super Bowl ended the following week. The 49ers lost to the Giants in overtime.

The Niners finished 11–4–1 in 2012. They raced through the playoffs to the Super Bowl. They faced the Baltimore Ravens. The Ravens flew to a 28–6 lead early in the third quarter. Then a power failure caused a half-hour delay. San Francisco surged back. But it was not enough. The Ravens won, 34–31. The next season, the 49ers went 12–4. They topped the Packers and the Carolina Panthers in

DEFENSIVE END JUSTIN SMITH

ALEX SMITH

DEFENSEMEN DEFOREST BUCKNER (NUMBER 99) AND RONALD BLAIR

the playoffs. They met the Seattle Seahawks in the NFC Championship Game. But San Francisco lost, 23–17.

The 49ers limped through the next few seasons. They started 2017 with nine straight losses. Then they acquired quarterback Jimmy Garoppolo. He started the final five games. San Francisco won them all. Fans looked forward to the future. Early in the 2018 season, a knee injury knocked Garoppolo out for the season. The 49ers fell to a disappointing 4–12 finish.

It took time for the San Francisco 49ers to find their footing in the NFL. Since then, they have rarely strayed from contention. They have five Super Bowl titles. "The City by the Bay" hopes it will soon host another championship celebration.

NFL CHAMPIONSHIPS

1981, 1984, 1988, 1989, 1994

SAN FRANCISCO 49ERS

https://www.49ers.com/

NFL: SAN FRANCISCO 49ERS TEAM PAGE

http://www.nfl.com/teams/sanfrancisco49ers/profile?team=SF

SAN FRANCISCO 49ERS

INDEX

COACH GEORGE SEIFERT WITH
MONTANA AND YOUNG